Coping with Children's Feeding F
Bedtime Battles

C000027462

-2 OCT

The PACTS series: *Parent, Adolescent and Child Training Skills*

Coping with Children's Feeding Problems and Bedtime Battles

by
Martin Herbert

BPS BOOKS   THE BRITISH PSYCHOLOGICAL SOCIETY

First published in 1996 by BPS Books (The British Psychological Society), St Andrews House, 48 Princess Road East, Leicester LE1 7DR, UK.

© Martin Herbert, 1996

This book is sold subject to the condition that it shall not, by way of trade or otherwise, be lent, resold, hired out, or otherwise circulated without the publisher's prior consent in any form of binding or cover other than that in which it is published and without a similar condition including this condition imposed on the subsequent purchaser.

A catalogue record for this book is available from the British Library.

ISBN 1 85433 193 0

Whilst every effort has been made to ensure the accuracy of the contents of this publication, the publishers and author expressly disclaim responsibility in law for negligence or any other cause of action whatsoever.

Typeset by Ralph Footring, Derby.

Printed in Great Britain by Stanley L. Hunt Printers Ltd., Rushden, Northants.

Contents

Coping with children's feeding problems and bedtime battles

Introduction

Two of the most common complaints made by parents faced with (or rather, confronted with) children who are apparently going through a defiant stage of development, concern 'battles' over eating and sleeping. The word 'battles' is apt, if unfortunate, as this is how hapless parents describe their seemingly endless struggles to get their child to eat properly, or to go to bed and stay there! Hence the title of this guide. Not infrequently such difficulties are linked in the same child, and are part of an overall pattern of oppositional behaviour.

How to survive and win

Paradoxically, I will suggest that the best way to survive and win these so-called battles is to stop thinking about them in these terms. Rather, think of them as situations in which children are trying to solve particular problems of their own, which, in turn, create problems which parents need to solve by a mixture of understanding, patience and some empirical knowledge-based strategies.

Aims

The aims of this guide are to provide the practitioner with:

1. a description of the main types of mealtime problem;
2. a guide to the assessment of mealtime difficulties;
3. a variety of mealtime behaviour management strategies and practical tips for encouraging the child to eat properly;
4. a description of bedtime 'battles' and 'ploys';
5. a guide to the assessment of bedtime difficulties (such as night waking, defiance at bedtime, leaving the bed at night, coming into the parents' bed, night-time fears and worries);
6. strategies for encouraging the child to remain in his/her own bed at night.

Caution

The advice in this guide is based upon the assumption that the child is physically well. Any suspicion that his/her behaviour or difficulties at night are associated with, or caused by, pain or illness, should lead you to seek prompt medical advice by a referral to the family doctor.

Part I: Behaviour problems at mealtimes

Typical mealtime difficulties include: bad table manners, refusing to eat or eating painfully slowly, getting up from the table, finicky eating habits, faddiness, throwing tantrums and crying. The family setting should (or could) provide an important opportunity for children to enjoy family life, and learn interactive skills; instead, it seems only too often (especially with pre-school children) to become the occasion for open warfare.

Prevalence (see also Douglas, 1989)

In a London study of the eating habits of a substantial cross-section of three-year-olds, 16 per cent were judged to have poor appetites, while 12 per cent were considered to be faddy. There were no sex differences in the rate of difficulties, but the problems were found to persist for one year in about two thirds of these children and to continue for over five years in about one third.

In a large-scale study of five-year-olds, over one third of the children were described as having mild or moderate appetite or eating problems. Two thirds of these were considered to be faddy eaters, while the remainder were thought not to eat enough.

Origins

Personality theorists (notably the Freudians) have always emphasized the importance of early satisfying feeding experiences in the development of personality traits (for example, what he called 'oral' optimism vs. pessimism) and parent–child relationships. During the early weeks after birth, most of an infant's waking hours involve feeding, and this is an important component of the bonding process between parent and child. While it is not contentious to suggest that the development of positive feeding patterns is significant to the child's physical and psychological well-being, the fuss made by early theorists about the long-term effects of scheduled vs. unscheduled feeding or early vs. late weaning on personality development proved to be unjustified. However, this is not to say it is not important to make an infant's feeds as relaxed and pleasant an occasion as possible.

Parents frequently make of mealtimes (like bedtime) a rod for their own backs by failing early on to establish routines which are (as habits) the means to put the child on autopilot at such times. They may give the child too much choice. There may be too many distractions, such as TV or family rows. They may have little idea about how much the child's appetite matches the helpings on the plate, thus provoking conflict when the child picks at his/her food or refuses to empty the plate.

Problems surrounding eating and food often arise out of difficulties in relationships in general; likewise, difficulties in relationships may stem from eating/feeding problems – sometimes originating in an organic disorder such as pyloric stenosis (narrowing of the muscular outlet of the stomach). The temperament of the child may clash with that of the parent and mealtime problems thus occur in the context of a wide range of other management problems. The child may be very defiant and self-willed and the parents may not have learned how to cope with the child's disruptive behaviour generally.

Types of mealtime/feeding problems

A wide range of eating difficulties is described by parents; their severity can range from simple feeding problems to failure to thrive due to emotional abuse or insufficient nutrition. Parents can become very worried about slight losses of appetite in their child while others may not notice that their child is malnourished.

Finicky eating

Parents differ in the amounts of food they expect children to eat or need nutritionally. Growth charts (see p. 6) are more reliable than arbitrary labelling of the child as a 'poor' or 'finicky' eater, as almost every child becomes finicky about food at some time. At some ages, this is simply a matter of disliking certain tastes or textures, or being more interested in experimenting, playing and talking than eating. However, some children learn to be fussy after observing other family members who are finicky.

Disruptive behaviour

Disruptive mealtime behaviours can include stealing food from others, eating spilled food, aggressiveness towards others at the table, destructive acts such as throwing food, drink, plates and cutlery, screaming and throwing tantrums.

Childhood psychological problems

Anxiety, depression or reactions to adverse (perhaps abusive) relationships within the family may cause the child to stop eating and thus fail to thrive. What do we mean by psychological problems? From the parents' (and, indeed, teachers') perspective, they tend to become worried about the children in their care when their behaviour appears (a) to be out of control; (b) to be unpredictable; or (c) to lack sense or meaning. If these tendencies are extreme and/or persistent they are likely to be thought of as 'problematic' or 'abnormal', and the growing concern they engender may result in a referral (usually through a social worker or general practitioner) to a clinical child psychologist or child psychiatrist. What sort of behaviours cause most concern? Achenbach and Edelbrock (1983) collected data on 2300 children referred to 42 mental health settings, based upon the parents' observations of the children in their care. The *Child Behaviour Checklist* (CBCL) was used for this purpose. Statistical analysis of scores uncovered several syndromes (clusters), which could be described by two broad categories: 'internalizing' behaviours and 'externalizing' behaviours. The former included emotional problems such as anxiety, phobias, inhibitions, fearfulness, worrying, and somatic difficulties, while the latter included aggression, fighting, noncompliance and hyperactivity. What is impressive is that these behaviour clusters suggesting a category of excess approach behaviour (antisocial aggression) and excess avoidance behaviour (inhibition/social withdrawal), have emerged in several empirical studies conducted on children in a variety of schools, child guidance clinics and residential institutions.

It is the externalizing problems which are most commonly associated with the feeding and bedtime problems where resistance is most evident; and it is the internalizing problems which sometimes form a backdrop to the difficulties which involve anxiety and fear.

Non-organic failure to thrive

This is a term used to describe infants and children whose growth and development are significantly below age-related norms and in whom no physical causes can be detected. These children frequently appear to be withdrawn, depressed, lethargic, anxious, whiny and tearful. These problems are frequently the outward and physical signs of emotional abuse and/or neglect (see Iwaniec, 1995; Iwaniec, Herbert and Sluckin, 1988).

In severe cases of failure to thrive, admission to hospital provides an environment where close observation of feeding patterns and mother–child interactions can occur. A treatment programme is described in *Appendix II* on p. 30.

Assessment of feeding problems

Keeping a food diary

Parents are asked to keep a detailed record of what exactly the child eats over the course of a day, or, if possible, a week. This should include details of the amount and type of food eaten, including all snacks and drinks, as well as the time and place. This record is particularly important where obesity is a problem. A precise record of the quantity of food eaten is critical.

Height and weight charts

Height and weight records are useful in assessment and treatment as they aid the practitioner in deciding on the health implications of the child's eating problem. If there are concerns about the child's health, check with a paediatrician to ensure that the weight-for-height is within normal limits. Remember not to judge adequate nutrition by how much is eaten since there are wide differences in the amount of food children require. Just as language or motor development progresses in stops and starts, so do growth, weight gain and appetite. At certain ages, children have less need for calories. Between the ages of one and five, most children gain four to five pounds a year but many will go three to four months without any weight gain at all, resulting in a decline in appetite.

Questionnaire assessment

The following questions put to caregivers should provide you with useful assessment data.

QUESTIONNAIRE: Mealtime Behaviour

(1) *Do you have rules about mealtime behaviour (e.g. manners) which you want your child to follow at home?*

(2) *What are they?*
> If only requirements are stated, question the caregiver further about prohibitions and encouraging strategies. If many are mentioned, ask only for the most important.

(3) *List in order the five most important rules to be followed.*
> Interviewer may need to 'remind' parent of listed rules.

(4) *How is the existence of these rules or expectations conveyed to your child?*
> If the answer is that they are conveyed verbally, probe to see if this occurs only when the rule is broken.

(5) *Taking each of the five most important rules in turn, ask why it is important for the child to follow that rule.*

(6) *Does ... have the same mealtime rules for your child?*
> Insert the name of the father or other caregiver above.

(7) *How often is each rule broken?*
> For each of the five important rules, obtain estimates in terms of average number of times per week.

(8) *What happens when the child breaks these rules?*
> Take each of the five important rules in turn and probe for:
> (i) consequences
> (ii) consistency across time
> (iii) consistency across adults
> (iv) whether or not a rationale is given

(9) *What happens when the child follows the mealtime rules?*

(10) *Do you have the same rules for all children in the family?*

(11) *Ask the reason for the answer given to question 10.*

(12) *Have you ever sought help from anyone for the management of any of your children's feeding/eating behaviours?*
> If the answer is yes, ask who was consulted, for which child, and get a brief account of what happened.

Observation

Sit in (if you can) on a meal and watch from the sidelines how the child and others behave, what is said, the emotional 'climate', the type of food served, helping sizes, and so on. A detailed observation of the parent feeding the very young child can give a guide to the emotional nature of the relationship. For example, a parent's brusqueness or lack of enthusiasm can lead to the child feeling frustrated and angry. The child may refuse food or be reluctant to eat, causing anger in the parent who interprets it as the child acting up and being naughty.

Then again, mealtimes may set the stage for disruption to occur, with children running around and not coming to the table to eat. The parents may become very angry and frustrated, shouting at the children and adding to the general high level of tension and disturbance.

An over-intrusive mother or father can also affect the child's feeding. Not allowing the child independence for self-feeding or for getting messy can interfere with normal developmental learning. The parent's anxiety will be communicated to the child, causing distress and, perhaps, a refusal to eat.

Organic factors

Congenital abnormalities of the intestinal tract, the existence of neuromotor dysfunctions, and ill health all influence or cause eating problems and/or loss of appetite. These require medical attention.

The child's appetite

It is necessary to take account of a child's level of appetite in any assessment of mealtime difficulties. Adults have usually been reared in a tradition of three meals a days, but this is not necessarily the schedule that best fits the *young* child's feeding needs. Most young children require four to five small meals a day: morning, mid-morning, noon, mid-afternoon and evening. This affects food helping sizes – a mid-afternoon snack may make a substantial dinner redundant. Parents need reminding that children do not necessarily have the same appetite as themselves, and there is nothing more off-putting than a mountain of food on one's plate that one **must** eat up! It is much better to give children a modest helping and the opportunity to come back for more. On the other hand, there's nothing more irritating than spending time preparing an attractive and nutritious meal only to have it rejected.

In psychodynamic theorizing, there is a symbolic (and indeed actual) relationship between food and love (also nurturance). Thus the rejection of food from a parent may be interpreted as the rejection of their care and affection.

Responsive/unresponsive parenting

In some families, the child with the feeding problem may be the one who has had long-standing behavioural or emotional difficulties since birth, or from soon afterwards. The interactions between parents and children, particularly the early ones involving communication between mother and baby, are *crucial* to the child's health and well-being. What a baby needs in order to develop vigorously is a close, confident and caring physical and emotional contact with the parent, be it mother (or mother-surrogate), father, or both. The absence of such continuing nurturance and physical intimacy can bring about anxiety, fretting, and disruption of the child's biological functions. One of the indices of basic trust and security in an infant is stable feeding behaviour. Parental responsiveness and sensitivity are vital in facilitating this (see Proforma in *Appendix I*).

An acute feeding difficulty that persists over a considerable time results not only in the child's poor growth and development but also, in some circumstances, leads to distortions of the mother–child relationship or exacerbates already existing difficulties – a 'chicken–egg' conundrum to be disentangled by the practitioner.

Environmental stresses on the caregiver

Marital difficulties, single parenthood, interfering and critical relatives all contribute to the undermining of a parent's confidence in managing their child. For example, a mother suffering from depression is unlikely to 'tune in' to her child in a sufficiently sensitive manner to be able to construct with him/her a mutually beneficial and stimulating sequence of interaction, the kind that enhances early feeding experiences.

Part II: Managing mealtime behaviour

Jo Douglas (1989) recommends a mixture of behaviour management skills, nutritional help, reassurance, confidence-building and monitoring, in the task of helping parents cope with feeding difficulties. Behavioural methods have a proven track record (see Herbert, 1987; 1994). For instance, children learn much of their behaviour by observing how parents react, and this also applies to mealtime situations. They learn from noticing how their parents eat, talk and behave at the table. They watch with interest how their father receives their mother's suggestion that he put down his newspaper during the meal, or stop gulping his meal. Does Dad sulk, get angry or co-operate?

Teaching parents behavioural methods

Here, briefly, are some disciplinary tactics (behavioural methods) which you can encourage parents to think about for themselves in relation to their children in various situations.

Stimulus control

Parents may need help in establishing the *setting cues* associated with eating. Simple guidelines about only eating at the table at meal-times and having a special place-mat for a young child help to establish cues, routines and habits for eating appropriately.

Positive reinforcement

If we wish to help children unlearn unwanted mealtime behaviours and learn something more appropriate in their place, we must change the way in which they are rewarded or not rewarded for their actions. This we refer to as 'reinforcement training'. Following is one of the questions to think through with parents which will help generate treatment strategies based on positive reinforcement.

Are you making good behaviour worthwhile?

Some parents remember to reward ('reinforce') desirable feeding behaviour. We need to think about a new slogan: 'Catch the child out in *good* mealtime behaviour rather than always in bad behaviour'. This means that if we have been rewarding inappropriate behaviour with attention (angry or otherwise), and ignoring, for the most part, good behaviour, then we must reverse our reactions and start ignoring the inappropriate behaviour as much as is feasible, and reward the good. This sounds simple enough, but of course it raises all kinds of questions and potential complications (see Herbert, 1987).

To have most effect, reinforcers such as treats, favoured activities, praise and encouragement should follow as closely as possible upon the child's performance of the particular desired mealtime behaviour. Thus the parent who sensitively monitors his/her children and is quick to draw attention to modest success (such as simply eating quietly), is using praise and encouragement more effectively than the parent who only gives favourable comments when, for example, the child does something quite extraordinary.

The 'praise–ignore' formula

The differential use of attention (for example, praise) and ignoring is widely advocated as an early step in behavioural interventions within families and school settings. It is particularly pertinent if the child is not receiving enough positive reinforcement (attention) and/or is receiving it at inappropriate times. The attention rule states that a child will work for attention from others, especially parents. If the child is not receiving positive attention, s/he will work to receive negative attention. Mind you, there are some children who are not very responsive, and indeed, appear counter-reactive, to what adults think of as positive attention. Why this should be requires an assessment of the quality of the interactions. Table 1 provides a rough and ready rule of thumb for linking behaviour and reinforcement.

Table 1. Links between behaviour and reinforcement

Acceptable behaviour	+ reinforcement (reward)	= more acceptable behaviour
Acceptable behaviour	+ no reinforcement	= less acceptable behaviour
Unacceptable behaviour	+ reinforcement (reward)	= more unacceptable behaviour
Unacceptable behaviour	+ no reinforcement	= less unacceptable behaviour

A prerequisite for parent mealtime behavioural programmes is thought by many to be an assurance that parents *can* provide meaningful, positive attention to the child in a manner that is consistent, while ignoring inappropriate actions. It goes without saying that if children love, trust and respect their parents – in other words, *identify* with them – their desire to please them makes parents' rewards and sanctions very powerful. 'Affection is a premium fuel for learning' is a useful axiom for parents with resistive children.

Some parents make undesirable behaviour unworthwhile, as outlined in Table 2.

Table 2. Making undesirable behaviour unworthwhile

	Antecedents	Behaviour	Consequences
(a)	Jason wanted to play with his computer game rather than eat his meal. Dad said there wasn't time before tea.	Jason kicked and shouted, lay on the floor and screamed.	Dad ignored his tantrum; eventually Jason calmed down and began to eat at the table.
(b)	Nisha was having breakfast.	She kept throwing food on the floor.	Mum, after one warning, took away her breakfast and Nisha had to go hungry.

Just as behaviour that is reinforced tends to recur, so behaviour that is not reinforced (example a) or punished (example b) tends to be discontinued. It is important to reassure parents that by 'rewards' we are not referring to expensive, tangible things, and that by 'punishments' we are not denoting things that are physical, harsh or painful. We are trying to help children to see that certain behaviours produce desirable consequences when eating/sitting at the table, while other forms of behaviour do not.

These methods are particularly useful when the child is on a difficult diet (for whatever medical reason) and is resisting the regime.

The child on a diet

Parents should keep a 'good behaviour' (see pp. 33 and 34) and weight chart for the child who is dieting so that s/he can see their progress or failure and the aim of treatment is kept in mind. Placing the chart on the fridge door may encourage parents not to indulge their child where there is an issue of compliance in the case of the child's obesity. Overweight children often have few limits set for their general behaviour or for their eating habits.

Ignoring

There is little doubt that attention, whether positive or negative, can be a very powerful reinforcer for children's behaviour. Inappropriate eating habits in children who are able to feed themselves may be the result of limited skills or poor motivation. However, in many cases, disruptive mealtime behaviours and improper table habits are effective means of gaining 'pay offs' in the form of attention. This gives rise to the question: 'Why does the child need to behave badly to get attention? Is not enough attention given at other times, especially when s/he behaves well?' Frequently, parents' reprimands and attempts to clean up the mess on the table and/or attempts to clean the child after a meal can reinforce the behaviour.

Time-out

Various disruptive mealtime behaviours contain elements of attention-seeking, but cannot be ignored. Time-out is a procedure which may reduce such problems. This method involves removing the child from the rewarding situation related to the problem behaviour, for example, to a 'time-out' chair in a corner. Alternatively, the source of the provocation may be removed when the misbehaviour occurs, for example, removal of the child's food which s/he has been spitting out. At the same time, attention should be withdrawn.

To be effective, time-out needs to be applied:

➢ consistently – whenever the problem behaviour occurs;
➢ immediately – so that the time-out is associated directly with the problem behaviour;
➢ with minimal attention or fuss – the child or food should be removed without comment and in a perfunctory manner. Remember that both angry and amused responses can be rewarding;
➢ for short periods of time – two to five minutes, supervised;
➢ in conjunction with praise and attention for appropriate behaviour when time-out is not in use.

Time-out is meant to be a mild form of punishment and is therefore ineffective if removal from the meal is in itself rewarding. For example, children may be happy to be removed from a meal which they don't want to eat. The success of time-out depends upon:

> ➤ the lack of reward value, interest or stimulation, in the time-out situation;
> ➤ the reward value of the situation from which the child is removed; or
> ➤ the reward value of the food removed from the child.

Care should be taken to give positive reinforcement for appropriate behaviour. It is crucial to develop *positive* behaviours to replace disruptive ones.

Natural or logical consequences

These can be explained to parents as follows.

Although you can't force your children to eat at mealtimes, you can have control over what they eat between meals. Hunger is a natural consequence of not eating, so use it to your advantage. Explain to your children, 'If you don't eat your lunch by the time the timer rings, I'll take away your plate and there won't be any snacks until dinner'.

Part III: Behaviour problems at bedtime

Let us begin with an admission. The experts still don't fully understand why people need to sleep or what purpose sleep serves. But we all *need* our sleep! And this statement is particularly poignant for those parents whose sleep is disrupted by a child with persistent bedtime problems. What we do know is that night-time difficulties are among the most common problems confronting parents.

Prevalence

Naomi Richman's 1981 survey of 771 children with sleep disruption problems (cited in Douglas and Richman, 1985) found that as many as ten per cent in one- to two-year-olds had severe, that is, problematic, rates of waking. Bedtime problems are also among the most common problems in older children as well.

The sleep cycle

An infant's pattern of sleeping is as individual as the uniqueness of his/her developing personality. This basic 'sleep cycle', as it is known, is programmed – a biological given (not learned), and as such, cannot be altered by parents or the baby. It is biologically regulated by a system of neurones situated in the core of the brain, and in the first half year of life or so, the pattern of sleeping reflects the child's individual biological development. Nevertheless, this is no reason for inaction; parents can begin gradually to instil routines – the foundation stones of good sleeping habits – and their expectations can have a powerful influence on how their child's sleep routines develop as s/he gets older. It is best to avoid labels such as 'She's a poor sleeper', or 'He needs hardly any sleep'. If parents assume that the child is incapable of changing and they act on such an assumption, the 'self-fulfilling prophecy' will come into play and they could allow their child to develop poor sleep habits.

Richard Ferber (1985), a distinguished researcher into sleep problems, says this:

> Because … parents were led to believe their child was just a poor sleeper and there wasn't anything they could do about it, they allowed their baby to develop poor sleep habits; they did not believe there was anything they could do to help him develop good ones. As a result the whole family suffered terribly. Yet I have found that almost all of these children are potentially fine sleepers and with just a little intervention can learn to sleep well.

Here then, is an optimistic message! A good starting point for us is to look briefly at the nature of sleep and the range of night-time problems.

When is a problem a problem?

Given that many children have occasional sleeping/bedtime problems, when can one say that a problem is really a problem? Here is a practical consideration: are the particular difficulties associated with bedtime **frequent, intense, numerous** and of **long duration**? Let us look at each of these characteristics in turn.

Frequency: Do the problems occur often? Does the child get out of bed every night? Come to their parents' bed several times during the night?

Intensity: Is the child very fearful of the dark? Does s/he have tantrums when asked to get ready for bed?

Number: Are there several kinds of bedtime problems, such as nightmares, plus coming to the parents' bed, plus bedwetting? Are there other behaviour problems, for example, defiance, aggression?

Duration: Has the problem persisted for a long time?

Another consideration is the question of what actually is 'normal' sleep.

'Normal' sleep patterns

Going back to the very beginning, the foetus in the womb is thought not to be truly awake, but alternating between **active** sleep and **quiet** sleep. Newborn (full term) babies spend some 75 per cent of each 24-hour period asleep. They usually have, on average, about eight periods of sleep a day, often in snatches, and the length of period varies from baby to baby. Newborns typically sleep for two to four hours at a time (note the wide range!). Their need for sleep also varies widely: from 11 to 21 hours in any 24-hour period. By six months of age, babies are spending some 50 per cent of each 24-hour period asleep.

Night waking

Brief periods of night waking are quite usual in infancy; by the end of the first month most babies are waking up twice a night to eat. Two-month-old infants spend, on average, some nine per cent of the night's sleeptime actually awake; by nine months of age the time awake reduces to about six per cent. Infants usually settle themselves and go back to sleep again, although sometimes they cry out. The extent to which parents are conscious of infants' waking depends on whether s/he sleeps with them, how often they monitor whether the child is asleep, and their sensitivity to crying.

Types of sleep

Sleep is not a *single* state distinguishable from the waking state; it is *two* very different states:

➤ REM or Rapid Eye Movement sleep: an **active** period of sleep when we do our dreaming; and

➤ non-REM sleep – the kind we usually think of as 'sleep', a quiet, deeper kind of sleeping without body or eye movements. Most of the restorative functions of sleep occur in this phase; there is little, if any, dreaming and there is a regular pattern of breathing and heart-rate.

REM sleep appears in the foetus at about six or seven months' gestation, and non-REM sleep between seven and eight months. At birth, a full-term baby will have 50 per cent of its sleep in REM state (premature babies 80 per cent); 35 per cent by age three; and 25 per cent for late childhood, adolescence and adulthood. REM sleep thus seems most important in the early months as the foetus and baby develop. Babies make frequent transitions between the two states and during the periods of light/active sleep a baby is easily awakened. About half of a newborn baby's sleep (as we have seen) is spent in each of these active vs. quiet states. As children mature they develop at their own pace the ability to pass through periods of light sleep more rapidly.

Nursing and rocking help a baby enter the deeper, quiet phase of sleeping. Some babies sleep relatively little; many need more sleep, but they will get all the sleep they need provided they are not left hungry, are not in pain, or not constantly interrupted. The two-month-old, on average, may need 27 minutes to drop off.

Daytime napping

The move from round-the-clock sleeping to a daytime napping schedule happens largely on its own. By the second month, infants are awake more during the day. By the third to sixth month parents' lives are enjoying some regularity again, as the baby may have developed a routine of two longer daytime sleeps. Many babies don't sleep through the night until they are six months old. At this age a majority (83 per cent) do so.

One can encourage the transition to a daytime napping schedule by putting a baby down between 8 and 10 a.m. and 1 or 2 p.m. Some time during the second year there is a transition to the single afternoon sleep, and by four years of age children may not feel the need of a nap.

The older child

Night waking is still common in the older child; only about 50 per cent of all toddlers sleep through the night at the age of two. By this age, most children are taking just one nap a day, usually after lunch. Going to bed may become a problem with a wilful toddler, and keeping him/her there may be an added ingredient of misery for parents. Some children simply aren't sleepy when their parents think they should be, while others fight sleepiness as if it is the enemy!

One cannot legislate for when a child falls asleep, but one can establish (early on, preferably) a pleasant routine for when s/he goes to bed. The bedtime ritual is a particularly powerful habit; a regular routine of meal, bath and then a story before bed makes the child's world seem well-ordered, safe and comfortable. It is not trivializing to set up these routines. Psychologists and social workers who visit chaotic homes where there is no certainty, regularity and routine know how disturbing this is to young children. It is also not helpful to older ones when they enter the relatively orderly life demanded at school.

How much sleep is necessary?

Before considering some ideas about how to put a child to bed and encouraging him/her to stay there, parents need to feel confident about how much sleep s/he needs. The following figure (adapted from Ferber, 1985) is an *approximate* guide only, as children vary in their need for rest.

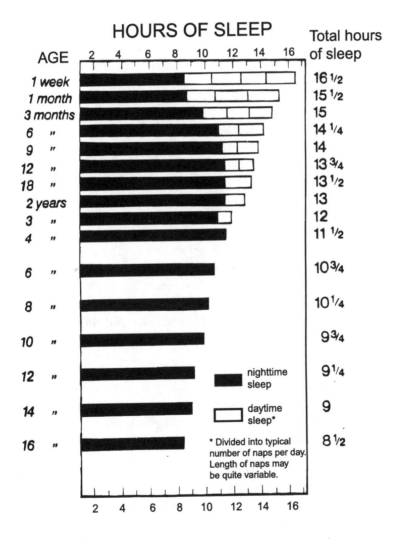

Figure 1. Typical sleep requirements in childhood (adapted from Ferber, 1985).

Part IV: Assessment

Bedtime battles and ploys

In some homes going to bed or going to sleep (whatever the time) is a struggle for control, continuing from the child's earliest years through to the school years. A detailed assessment of the child's sleep pattern and bedtime behaviour, and also of the parents' management strategies, is essential for an effective plan of treatment to be worked out in partnership with the parents.

The bedtime problem may take one of four forms. For example:

➤ **The bedtime battle**: Here the child flatly refuses to go to bed at the allotted time and defies all requests/instructions/pleas/demands to go to bed by ignoring/arguing/running away/or throwing a violent temper tantrum.

➤ **The bedtime 'game'**: In this variety the child dreams up a variety of ploys to delay bedtime: for example, needing just a few more minutes to see a TV programme; needing to say good night to all the pets in the house; wanting just one more story; needing to go to the toilet yet again or have another drink of water; suddenly remembering something important to tell Mum and so on. Some children develop incredibly elaborate and time-consuming rituals in which parents have to play their intricate part before the child will go to sleep.

➤ **The 'summons'**: Some children may go to bed readily, but later repeatedly ask for parents to come to them, escalating into a form of emotional blackmail by crying or screaming if the summons is not obeyed.

➤ **Coming to parents' bed**: For a variety of reasons children fall into the habit of getting into their parents' bed. Even when fear is not involved it can be a difficult habit to break. It may seem obvious that a simple, structured and persistent strategy will get the child to stay in his/her room, and yet many resourceful parents tell us that this problem defeats them.

The line of least resistance

Parents sometimes, from sheer exhaustion and despair, let the child stay up until s/he falls asleep in the sitting room. The child is then carried to bed where the confrontation is quite likely to begin all over again. Some parents sit for ages by the child's bed until s/he falls asleep. Others accede to the demand that the child sleeps in Dad and Mum's bed, and perhaps even end up going to bed early for the sake of 'peace and quiet'.

What parents are unwittingly teaching their children is that their coercive actions, be they refusals, temper tantrums or 'cunning ploys', if sufficiently intense and/or prolonged, will in the end get them their own way.

Bedtime/sleep diaries (see *Appendix III*)

To understand exactly what is happening you will need some detailed information. Asking parents to keep a bedtime behaviour and sleep diary provides a picture of the child's sleep pattern and is vital in planning an effective intervention. Some children will play up at bedtime. Some will still be having daytime naps which interfere with a prolonged sleep at night, so the pattern over twenty-four hours is helpful. The chart records the total time that the child is awake during the night, including the frequency of waking and the duration of time awake; also what s/he does on waking – for example, coming to the parents' bed, and the parents' reactions to the waking behaviour.

Routines

In conducting an assessment it is important to remember that children who refuse to go to bed or who wake early are often responding to inappropriate cues about how they are expected to behave (Douglas, 1989). Getting ready for bed may have become disconnected from actually going to bed and falling asleep. There can be a gap of several hours of play between getting changed and falling asleep. The cues for falling asleep may be linked to the parents going to bed.

The child needs to learn a set routine which is relatively brief (up to half an hour) of getting ready for bed and falling asleep. A regular and relatively brief sequence of wash, change, drink, story, song, and cuddle enables the child to calm down and learn the next stage in the pattern. The parents need to be *consistent* in their approach to bedtime. A detailed history of the child's bedtime problem and the parents' management style will often reveal the parents' use of different ideas and methods. For example, parents may have tried a strategy for a time but given up too quickly.

Part V: Night-time fears and worries

There are times when children say they do not want to go to bed, or wish to come through to their parents during the night, because they are afraid of the dark, of being left alone, or some other thing. *All* children experience fear during their development; one- and two-year-olds show a range of fears, including separation from parents and fear of strangers. During the third and fourth years of life, fear of the dark, of being left alone, and fear of small animals and insects emerge. Fears of wild animals, ghosts and monsters come to the fore during the fifth to sixth years; and fears of school, supernatural events, and physical dangers emerge in the seventh and eighth years. During the ninth to eleventh years, social fears and fears of war, ill-health, bodily injury, and school performance become more prominent.

These are age-related tendencies and it is possible to see how some of them might be related to anxieties about going to bed – fear of the dark, ghosts, being alone. Some children lie awake at night worrying about school, about death, about their own or their parents' health, and other concerns.

Fear of the dark

Many youngsters learn to fear the dark and this can cause bedtime problems. To be left in the dark is not initially an unpleasant experience for a young child, but sooner or later, however, when s/he is in pain with a tummy ache, frightened by a dream, hungry, cold or miserably wet, s/he will cry for Mum. She comes hot foot to the rescue, putting on the light as she enters the room, and soon comforts him/her in their distress. What better conditioning model could there be for unwittingly associating darkness with distress, and light with positive reinforcement in the form of a consoling mother?

What she might do is to enter the room without putting on the light, chatting and reassuring the child until she has ascertained the trouble, and then, if absolutely necessary, switching on the light to remedy the situation. This sequence of events ensures that there is no direct and recurrent relationship between the arrival or presence of mother and the light. If the child has learned to fear the dark because of terrifying tales from peers about ghosts and burglars, punishment is obviously quite inappropriate. At the back of this guide are some hints which can be given to parents.

Overcoming fear

The contagious effect of calmness and lack of fear has been used in extinguishing fears. Nursery school children who were afraid of dogs have been treated successfully during several brief sessions by observing unafraid children playing happily with a dog. The most effective methods used by adults to help their offspring are those which:

➤ help the child develop skills with which s/he can cope with the feared object or situation;

➤ take the child by degrees into active contact with the feared object or situation;

➤ give the child an opportunity gradually to become acquainted with the feared object or situation under circumstances that at the same time allow him/her the opportunity either to inspect or ignore it.

Methods that are sometimes helpful in enabling the child to overcome fears include:

➤ verbal explanation and reassurance;

➤ verbal explanation, plus a practical demonstration that the feared object or situation is not dangerous;

➤ giving the child examples of fearlessness regarding the feared object or situation (parents frequently quote the example of other children who are not afraid);

➤ conditioning the child to believe that the feared object is not dangerous but pleasurable.

Self-help

It has been found that children can overcome fears, either as part of the general process of growing up or by using the following techniques:

➤ practising overcoming their fear by enlisting the help of adults, imagining a partnership with fantasy characters such as Superman or favourite toys;

➤ talking with other people about the things they fear;

> arguing with themselves (following adult guidance) about the reality or unreality of dreaded imaginary creatures or fantasized events such as death, that they fear.

Bad dreams

Aggressive children tend to have more hostility in their dreams than gentle youngsters, and this can be frightening; anxious children have more unhappy, worrying dreams. Children who have been separated from their mother by a long stay in hospital, are more likely to be prone to nightmares subsequently, although there is no noticeable effect on the dreams of children who are separated from their mothers but remain in their own home. Unpleasant dreams tend to increase when a child is in poor health, with vivid nightmares about death, illness and other morbid topics.

Nightmares often set in following trauma such as bereavement or an accident. With minor trauma, they tend to be short periods when a child, particularly a sensitive child, appears unsettled or worried. The distress may arise from a change of school, a move to a new town or the stress of examinations. If a child is suffering from emotional problems, for instance not coming to terms with their parents' separation, or a new stepfather, s/he may have recurrent nightmares, often on a similar theme to the daytime worry. Disturbing dreams tend to become a particular problem for children around the ages of ten to eleven when one third or more experience them. For girls, nightmares show a peak in their incidence at six or seven years of age, becoming less frequent as they get older.

Part VI: Conclusions

Behavioural strategies (programmes) of the type described in this book have been shown to be effective in reducing many bedtime problems (see Herbert, 1991; 1994; Douglas and Richman, 1984, for a review of the evidence). One study of such methods was found to be successful in 90 per cent of children between one and five years old and the improvements were maintained over a four-month follow-up period. Another study based on the same format and carried out by health visitors found a 68 per cent improvement rate. Health visitors using a manual of behavioural techniques (Douglas and Richman, 1985) also found they could help parents improve their children's bedtime problems.

It is very important to be aware of three possible complications:

1. As already mentioned, if there is any hint of health problems playing a part in the child's sleep and bedtime problems, CONSULT THEIR GP.
2. A child's problems about being alone in the bedroom may have a basis in fear. See Part V on this.
3. The problem may be part of a more general and worrying problem of defiance. (A guide on this subject, *Banishing Bad Behaviour*, is also available).

There are several basic behavioural techniques that can be applied to the management of sleep disturbance (Douglas and Richman, 1984; 1995). Management advice is most effective when individually tailored to the needs of the family and the child. Parents need not be highly motivated to change their style of management for this approach to work effectively, but they have to be encouraged to express their views fully about what they think they can or cannot manage. Sleep problems and bedtime problems require a *partnership* between the parents and practitioner so that the most appropriate method can be chosen and enthusiastic co-operation for the exacting tasks ahead engendered.

References

Achenbach, T.M. and Edelbrock, C.S. (1983). Taxonomic issues in child psychology. In: T. Ollendick and M. Hersen (Eds) *Handbook of Child Psychopathology*. New York: Plenum.

Douglas, J. (1989). *Behaviour Problems in Young Children*. London: Tavistock/Routledge.

Douglas, J. and Richman, N. (1984). *My Child Won't Sleep*. Harmondsworth: Penguin.

Douglas, J. and Richman, N. (1985). *Sleep Management Manual*. London: Great Ormond Street Hospital for Sick Children.

Ferber, R. (1985). *Solve Your Child's Sleep Problems*. New York: Simon and Schuster.

Herbert, M. (1987). *Behavioural Treatment of Children with Problems*. London: Academic Press.

Herbert, M. (1991). *Clinical Child Psychology: Social Learning, Development and Behaviour*. Chichester: Wiley.

Herbert, M. (1994). Behavioural methods. In: M. Rutter *et al.*, *Child and Adolescent Psychiatry*. Oxford: Blackwell.

Iwaniec, D. (1995). *Emotional Abuse and Neglect*. Chichester: Wiley.

Iwaniec, D., Herbert, M., and Sluckin, A. (1988). Helping emotionally abused children who fail to thrive. In: K. Browne *et al.* (Eds) *Early Prediction and Prevention of Child Abuse*. Chichester: Wiley.

Further reading

Kitzinger, S. (1990). *The Crying Baby*. Harmondsworth: Penguin.

Lansky, V. (1991). *Getting Your Child to Sleep ... and Back to Sleep*. Deephaven: The Book Peddlers.

Schaffer, H.R. and Collis, G.M. (1986). Parental responsiveness and child behaviour. In: W. Sluckin and M. Herbert (Eds) *Parental Behaviour*. Oxford: Basil Blackwell.

Appendix I: Sensitive responsiveness to the infant

Child's name:
Child's age:
Date:

	Ratings			
Does the caregiver or parent:	Always	Most of the time	Some of the time	Never
Respond promptly to the infant's needs?				
Respond appropriately to his/her needs?				
Respond consistently?				
Interact smoothly and sensitively with the child?				

Prompt responding

Infants have very limited abilities to appreciate the contingencies (association) of events to their own behaviour; an interval of only three seconds is required to disrupt the contingency learning of six-month-old infants. Where the adult takes appreciably longer to answer the infant's signals there will be no opportunity for the child to learn that his/her behaviour can thereby affect his/her environment and in particular, the behaviour of other people.

Appropriate responding

This means the ability to recognize the particular 'messages' the infant is trying to communicate, and to interpret and react to them correctly.

Consistency

A child's environment must be predictable; s/he must be able to learn that his/her behaviour will produce particular consequences under particular conditions.

Interacting smoothly

Parents can mesh their interactions with the infant's in a manner that is facilitative and pleasurable as opposed to intrusive and disruptive.

Appendix II: A clinical treatment programme for children who fail to thrive

For details see Iwaniec *et al.* (1988).

Stage I

Feeding is tackled in a highly structured (and thus directed) manner. Mealtimes have to be made more relaxed. Mothers (and/or fathers) are asked (and rehearsed) to desist from screaming, shouting and threatening the child over meals (self-control training). The period of eating is made quiet and calm, and the parent is asked to talk soothingly and pleasantly to the child. It is extremely difficult for parents to achieve and maintain this pattern of behaviour and it is helpful if the practitioner models the feeding. The practitioner can feed the child a few times and then help to reassure the child; s/he may also have to prompt the mother to help the child, in a gentle manner, to eat, when they are in difficulties. The mother is encouraged to look at the child and to smile and touch him/her. If the child refuses food, the mother has to leave the child; if she can't encourage or coax him/her by play or soft words, arranging the food decoratively to look attractive helps. It is a bad idea for the parent to try to feed the child when feeling acutely tense or angry.

Stage II

This stage of the programme is discussed in detail; rationale and methods are explained to both parents. In most cases a contract is drawn up specifying the mutual obligations and rules for the family and practitioner. What might happen in situations where interactions are aversive is that the mother (and/or father) is encouraged to play exclusively with the child each evening for 10–15 minutes during the first week, for 15–20 minutes during the second and third weeks and 25–30 minutes during the fourth and subsequent weeks. After the mother's/father's session with the child, the rest of the family might join in for a family play session. The way the parent plays and the toys s/he uses, may have to be demonstrated and rehearsed with him/her. S/he should be encouraged to talk to the child in a soft, reassuring manner, commenting on his/her play, not directing it or taking it over.

The parent is also encouraged to smile at the child, look at them, hold their hand, stroke their hair and praise them for each positive response s/he gives. This may require successive approximations if his/her behaviour is very timid. The tentative approaches towards the parent are shaped by a series of reinforcements for these mini-steps towards the goal of seeking proximity to him/her. After a few days or even weeks (if interactions have been mutually aversive), the parent is guided to seek proximity to the child by hugging them briefly and holding them on their lap for increasing intervals of time, eventually holding them close but gently, while reading to them, looking at and describing pictures and so on.

This period of therapy requires a lot of support for the parent and for the whole family, and frequent visits and telephone calls should be made to monitor the programme. If there has been much rejection and/or hostility, it can take three months of hard work to bring a parent and child closer together to the point of beginning to enjoy being with each other.

Stage III

The final stage is planned to include two weeks of deliberately intensified parent–child interaction. The parent is to interact with the child as much as possible. S/he should chat to the child as much as possible, regardless of whether or not s/he fully understands what s/he is doing and saying. S/he should make a lot of eye contact, smile at them, cuddle them and hug them. This is a period of 'over-learning'. Apart from having them with him/her for everyday activities, s/he should spend time playing with all the children, encouraging the target child to participate in the play with their siblings. A bedtime story for all children might be introduced.

The formal programme is faded out gradually, over a period of several weeks. The case is terminated when there is evidence of the child's stable growth (measured by a paediatrician) and evidence of improved family interactions, maternal feelings and attitudes towards the child (these are always carefully monitored by a practitioner).

Appendix III. Baseline Assessment Recording Chart

Name:

Week beginning:

	Monday	Tuesday	Wednesday	Thursday	Friday	Saturday	Sunday
Time woke in morning							
Time of day naps							
Time went to bed							
Child's behaviour							
Parents' action/s							
Time went to sleep							
Times woke in night							
Child's behaviour							
Parents' action/s							
Time went to sleep again and where							

Appendix IV. Sunflower Chart

Colour in a flower for each task successfully achieved.

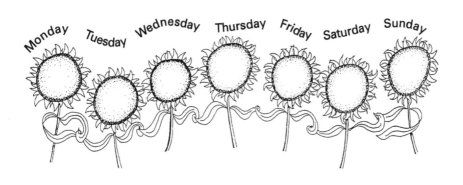

Appendix V: The Happy Face Chart

Draw a happy face for each task successfully achieved.

	Task			Week			Remarks
Monday							
Tuesday							
Wednesday							
Thursday							
Friday							
Saturday							
Sunday							

	Task			Week			Remarks
Monday							
Tuesday							
Wednesday							
Thursday							
Friday							
Saturday							
Sunday							

Hints for Parents 1: Coping with feeding problems

As parents we often tend to base the size of the helping or portion of food on what we think our children should eat, rather than on their actual needs or appetites. Children may not be hungry and resist having food forced upon them, so allow them to serve their own portions when possible. Giving them some say over the food that goes on their plates may reduce the conflict over how much enters their mouths. For very young children, it might be wiser to offer small portions, less than they are likely to want to eat. This will lead to a sense of accomplishment; and it is better to receive a request for an extra helping than a complaint that your child cannot or won't finish up what is on the plate.

Strategies to help your child eat

Offer limited choice

If your child is a faddy eater, resisting most of the usual family fare, s/he might be given the option of eating what the family eats, or instead, one type of nutritious food that they like. The choice should be made well before each meal, so that you are not forced into last-minute preparations. By offering an alternative, you give your child a face-saving way out of conflict.

A limited choice introduces the idea of compromise; offering choices indicates that you are willing to give your children some room to negotiate in a responsible way.

Reward good eating and table manners

As nagging and criticizing actually reinforce eating problems and encourage power struggles, you might find opportunities (without over-emphasizing) to praise another child who is behaving appropriately. For example, you could praise the child for staying seated, using cutlery properly and talking quietly. If and when a disruptive child is eating in the desired manner, you should be prompt in acknowledging the fact. You might say, 'You're doing so well by eating your dinner', or 'I'm really pleased that you can eat your food in such a grown-up way'.

When you pay attention to good manners rather than bad, children will learn that there is little pay-off for behaving badly.

Having time-limited meals

Some children drag mealtimes out by eating slowly, complaining at every mouthful and playing with their food. Instead of letting meals drag on and on, negotiate a reasonable amount of time in which the child has to finish eating, perhaps 20 to 30 minutes. Explain ahead of time that when a timer goes off, their plates will be removed. A star or sticker chart, where a star or sticker is awarded for eating well, should provide a powerful incentive if a scheme is established for the exchange of a certain number of stickers for a reward.

Hints for Parents 2: Coping with bedtime problems

Note to the practitioner

A choice of programmes to discuss with parents follows. You may wish to have them typed out or photocopied as handouts. It is not sufficient simply to give parents the instructions without carefully considering with them the practicalities (and potential difficulties) of each step; the means of problem-solving such setbacks; and (most crucially) tailoring the programme to the circumstances of the individual child and family.

The guidance given here is most effective when both parents (where there are two caregivers) agree about the rules for the child going to bed, and determine to be consistent in applying the programme and also to be firm, not punitive. The assumption for this strategy is that the chosen bedtime is a reasonable one for a child of his/her age, and that parents have arranged things so the timing is not in the middle of a favourite TV programme. A further assumption is that the child is sleeping in a separate room from the parent(s).

Careful clinical judgement is required before Strategy III is recommended or condoned. It may be inappropriate where the child is very anxious (see Part V of this guide), or where there is a situation of parental hostility and/or rejection.

Coping strategies for bedtime problems

In working out a reasonable bedtime, you will need to decide how much sleep your child needs. As the requirements are individual to the child, it is unhelpful to be too rigid (Figure A provides a general guide). For example, if you feel your six-year-old needs about ten hours of sleep and s/he usually gets up at 6.30 a.m., then his/her bedtime might be set at 8.30 p.m. The older the child, the more room there is for a degree of negotiation. Following are some useful strategies for handling bedtime problems.

Strategy I: Getting your child to bed

Step 1: Alert your child of the fact that bedtime is approaching about 15 minutes in advance (set a timer to announce it for a toddler).

Step 2: Arrange for it to be a quiet time before bedtime so your child isn't overstimulated. An excited, keyed-up child not only finds it hard to get to sleep, but also is more likely to wake during the night. Young children rarely possess the ability to calm themselves down. Rocking a toddler can be a pleasant way to end the day. Running-around games and frightening/exciting TV programmes are NOT helpful!

Step 3: Incorporate tooth-brushing, washing or bathing and putting pyjamas on into the bedtime routine.

Step 4: Tuck the child up into his/her own cot or bed. If a story is part of your usual routine, allow for this in your calculation of the amount of rest your child needs.

Step 5: If your child is restless and is having difficulties settling, here are some tips:

- ➤ Read some children's rhymes. The rhythm of poetry has a relaxing and soothing effect.
- ➤ Sing a lullaby to your child.
- ➤ Talk about what you'll be doing tomorrow. If it's something out of the ordinary to look forward to, say that the sooner the child falls asleep, the sooner tomorrow will come.
- ➤ Provide some form of comforter, such as a soft toy or blanket to cuddle.
- ➤ Turn on a cassette or record of soft, soothing music.

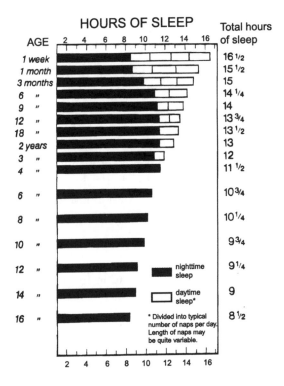

Figure A: Typical sleep requirements in childhood (adapted from Ferber, 1985).

Step 6: Tell the child you will see them in the morning, kiss them good night, turn off the light and leave the room.

There is another strategy which becomes necessary when a young child cannot or does not want to settle early in the evening, when you feel anxious about him/her, cannot stand to hear crying, or have difficulty in setting limits and boundaries to the child's behaviour. It requires planning a sequence of small changes that combine to reach the overall goal. A good example is the child who needs to be rocked or patted to sleep at bedtime and also every time they wake during the night. Once you have agreed to teach the child to fall asleep unaided, an outline of the different stages of settling can be negotiated. The pace set is designed so the child does not need to protest unduly and you can feel confident in the small limits that are being set. The starting-point will vary according to the pattern that each family has established when encouraging their child to settle to sleep.

BRITISH PSYCHOLOGICAL SOCIETY • PACTS SERIES • PACTS SERIES • BRITISH PSYCHOLOGICAL SOCIETY • PACTS SERIES • BRITISH PSYCHOLOGICAL SOCIETY

The following graded steps should be used for two or three nights each before moving on.

➢   Stand still and hold the child while s/he falls asleep.
➢   Sit down and hold the child.
➢   Place the child on a cushion on lap, still holding.
➢   Place the child in his/her cot, bend over the side and hold.
➢   Loosen hold while leaning over the cot side.
➢   Sit by the cot and hold hands through bars.
➢   Sit by the cot but don't touch the child.
➢   Sit away from the cot but don't look at the child.
➢   Sit out of sight in the bedroom.
➢   Stand by the bedroom door.
➢   Stand outside the door.

The process of gradual separation from the child involves parents being less responsive and having less physical contact.

Note for parents

Take turns going through the bedtime routine with your partner so your child won't come to insist that the same parent does it every night. In the toddler years when everything seems to meet with resistance, give positive choices whenever possible, such as, 'Do you want teddy or elephant to sleep with you tonight?'

Strategy II: When your child won't settle and stay in bed

Teaching your small son or daughter to go to sleep on his/her own may require considerable effort. The first few nights may well be exhausting, but with determination on your part the training process should work. The following points are important.

Step 1: Preparing for bed. This should be made a pleasant, reassuring time for your child, with a well-established time and routine.

Step 2: Preparing for sleep. This should occur with the child in bed. A story or two can be read together and you will probably wish to chat a little. Explanations of the new routine should be given at this time. The final part of this stage includes tucking him/her in, and a kiss, saying calmly but firmly: 'Good night, have a good sleep, see you in the morning'.

Step 3: During the first hours. If s/he cries or calls out ignore it – unless there is a note of urgency or panic – until s/he gets out of bed. If s/he does get out of bed and comes to the room where you are (and you have assured yourself that s/he is alright), take him/her back, without fuss, to the bedroom. Put him/her to bed in a matter-of-fact way. S/he should then be told, 'You must stay in bed: I have things to do. If you come out, I will take you right back'.

Step 4: This action needs to be repeated **consistently** whenever the child gets out of bed. Provide as little reinforcing attention (for example, chats and cuddles) as possible for these activities during the night.

Step 5: Pin up a 'bedtime chart' which is marked out in squares for every night of the week. If s/he does not get out of bed, tick the appropriate square and put a happy face or some other sticker on a star chart or let him/her colour in one section of a picture. Every success receives a lot of praise. Promise a special treat at the end of the week, such as having a friend to tea or an extra trip to the park, when the chart or picture is completed. The chart or picture is moved from his/her bedroom and pinned up in a place of honour in the sitting room. If s/he does get up on any night, you must repeat Steps 3 and 4 with **unremitting persistence**.

Strategy III: When your child wakes frequently and calls out or comes into your bed at night

In some cases children may go to bed and initially stay there quite happily. However, after they have been asleep for some time they suddenly wake up and call out or cry for you to come to them, usually soon after you have just fallen asleep. When this happens, they may stay awake for some time, and seriously disrupt your rest. For the child who continues to call, cry or come to your bed for 'wants' rather than 'needs', **crying it out** is the method you may have to use when all else fails, though not everybody agrees with this tough-minded method. After all, you have to learn to ignore the crying until the child falls asleep. Sometimes children can cry for hours if this method has failed previously and so you should be warned how difficult it may be. If you are particularly distressed by the crying, you can quickly check the child is safe, but you should not comfort or touch the child. Just tell him/her firmly to go to sleep. No prolonged debates!

This is a difficult method to use for some parents as the child can become very distressed and may make themselves sick with crying. You may have to go in to clean up the child and change the bedclothes, but this should be done with the minimum of fuss, and you should then put the child back to bed and walk out. If you choose to use this method, be warned that the problem can be made much worse if you do give in.

If you doubt your strength of resolve on any night, or have objections for ethical reasons, then you should not take it on.

Step 1: Before the child goes to bed, tell her/him that if they wake during the night they must stay in their own bed.

Step 2: (Calling out) If the first call is **not** one of distress, **IGNORE IT** (easier said than done, of course!). S/he may initially cry for some time, but if you give in and go to him/her after a while, they will learn that all they have to do is make a fuss loudly enough or long enough and Mummy or Daddy will come running.

Step 3: Ignore all ploys, if they are identified as such, namely unreasonable, attention-seeking, or manipulative requests. By ignoring I mean:
- no prolonged debates or chats;
- no drinks or food (have a glass of water or juice in the child's room);
- no entertainment (have some toys handy by the bed for the child to amuse him/herself with);
- no *obvious* worried monitoring (frequent visits to the child's room).

Step 4: (Coming to your bed) If your child leaves his/her bed for yours, return them **immediately** to their bed. Say nothing and **do not** cuddle or kiss them.

Step 5: Repeat this as often as is necessary. To begin with, your child will get up a lot, but if you are persistent and stick to this routine, you will win. It is important to get the child back into bed as soon as possible. A bell on his/her door will signal to you that s/he is leaving and enable you to intervene before s/he gets into your bed.

Step 6: In the morning, regardless of how many times s/he got up, tell them how grown up it was to have slept all night in their own bed. It is desirable to provide an incentive the following morning if the child stays in his/her own bed all night.

Strategy IV: A 'tender-minded' alternative

Some parents cannot face the distress they feel, or the distress they think the child feels as a result of the approach just described. They cannot let the child cry for a prolonged period, especially if they work themselves up into near-hysteria, so I suggest the following alternative.

Step 1: If you must go in, begin the process gradually. First wait a few minutes, rather than rushing in to calm your child.

Step 2: Give **minimal** attention! Tuck your child in; give only verbal assurances, including words to the effect that it's time to go to sleep and you'll see Mummy or Daddy in the morning. Touch the child briefly, perhaps a pat, but no prolonged conversation or cuddling.

Step 3: Be consistent and avoid the temptation to feed or hold your child.

Step 4: Simply visit your child at fifteen minute intervals for reassurance and a pat on the back (so s/he does not feel alone). Do not pick your child up or cuddle the child.

A variation on this strategy is to wait, say, three minutes after the first call; the next time five minutes; then ten minutes, 15 minutes and, gradually, eventually, no response.

While you may think that all of these procedures sound a little drastic, they are very often necessary to break long established habits of unco-operative bedtime behaviour. Much effort will initially be needed from you, especially in ignoring repeated cries for attention from the child's room. It may be a good idea to turn the volume on the television up, or put on some music to listen to as a distraction. It is often difficult to be firm; you will feel a mixture of emotions as you steel yourself to be consistent – guilt, anxiety, and (of course) exhaustion. But it is usually a worthwhile investment of time and energy. If the strategies are strictly followed by both parents, you are likely to find that success occurs within a few days. It is important that when your child *does* start to go to bed without a fuss, you tell them how pleased you are with them and how grown up they are.

Strategy V: Incentives (positive reinforcement)

With older children, actual and symbolic rewards (for example, points/stickers backed up by a success-orientated scheme of treats or tangible rewards) can be effective in encouraging appropriate bed-time behaviour. Certain questions are crucial to think through and they are presented below, along with a discussion of the treatment strategies they might generate.

Question 1: Are you making good bedtime behaviour worthwhile?

Some parents *remember* to reward ('reinforce') desirable bedtime behaviour as shown in the following example:

Antecedents	Behaviour	Consequences
Marie was asked to put away her toys and go to bed.	She did so.	Her mum gave her a big hug and said thank you.

Comment: Because of the social reward given by her mother, Marie is likely to go to bed when asked again. Can you think of what bedtime behaviour you would particularly wish to encourage, strengthen or increase in frequency in your child? In order to improve or increase your child's performance of certain actions, you could think about how to arrange matters so that a reinforcing event (it might be an activity your child enjoys) follows the correct performance of the desired behaviour. You might say, for example, '**When** you have put your pyjamas on and get into bed, **then** you can have a story and a sticker in your merit book'. This is the useful 'when–then' rule (sometimes referred to as the 'first–then' rule).

Question 2: Are you making desirable bedtime behaviour unworthwhile?

Some parents *forget* to reward ('reinforce') desirable bedtime behaviours as shown in the following example.

Antecedents	Behaviour	Consequences
Toby made a bargain to go to bed in future without a tantrum.	Toby was reluctant but kept to his bargain the next night, without a fuss.	His mother showed no recognition of his honouring his bargain.

Comment: Toby is likely to go back on his bargain in future. Do you, perhaps for what seem like good reasons, such as being too busy, fail to notice when your child is being co-operative and obedient? You don't have to make long speeches or give rewards. Signs of pleasure on your part, a word of praise, usually work wonders.

Question 3: Are you making undesirable bedtime behaviour worthwhile?

Some parents persistently overlook or ignore their children's undesirable bedtime actions, inadvertently allowing them to be reinforced by circumstances, as in the following example.

Antecedents	Behaviour	Consequences
Father asked Denise to go upstairs to bed.	She ignored his requests.	Nil. Mother made no comments; father shrugged his shoulders and said, 'What's the use?'

Comment: It won't be surprising if Denise doesn't take any notice next time around. After all she has got her way. Do you fail sometimes to notice or sanction your child's unacceptable actions? The best outcomes are obtained when you use both praise for obedience and a penalty for disobedience.

Strategy VI: Applying a sanction: response–cost

The use of response–cost procedures involves a penalty being given when a child doesn't obey. This may involve giving up rewards currently available, as, for example, when failure to stay in bed results in the loss of television privileges.

In the following case, a hyperactive boy, Barry, was extremely disruptive and noisy at bedtime, coming downstairs repeatedly from his bedroom. He made life miserable for his parents, who spent hours taking him back to bed, arguing with him, or (more often) giving into him so that he ended up going to bed half-asleep, when they went to bed.

The response–cost method was explained to his parents in the following way: 'To stop Barry from acting in an unacceptable way, you need to arrange for him to bring to an end a **moderately** (but significantly) unpleasant situation immediately by changing his behaviour in the desired direction'. The parents worked out the following scenario for Barry.

A bottle of marbles representing his weekly pocket money plus a bonus was placed on the mantelpiece. Each instance of misbehaviour (coming downstairs) 'cost' a marble (the equivalent of a specific sum of money). In a good week, Barry could increase his pocket money quite substantially; in a bad week it could be reduced to zero. Of course, the 'cost' of transgressions was highly visible to the boy. As always, sanctions were to be balanced by rewards – a special treat if he refrained from coming down for several nights in a week. Punishment alone tells children what *not* to do, not what they *are* expected to do.

FACTS SERIES • BRITISH PSYCHOLOGICAL SOCIETY • FACTS SERIES • BRITISH PSYCHOLOGICAL SOCIETY

Hints for Parents 3: Fear of the dark

If your child is scared of the dark and comes to your bedroom during the night, first of all you might leave the bedroom light on for him/her to get to sleep, switching it off when s/he is asleep, and leaving the door open with a light on outside so that s/he will not wake up in total darkness. Each night move the light gradually further towards the door and out of the room. (If you have one, use a dimmer switch to achieve this gradual process.) To avoid sudden distress on the child's part you could explain it to them as a 'game'. Make sure that s/he knows how to switch on the light him/herself should s/he wake up and want it on. When they fall asleep you can again turn the light off. Because the situation is under the child's control there will be no call for panic. Given sufficient patience on your side, your child will eventually get tired of leaving the comfort of his/her bed in order to switch on the light, and will decide (hopefully) that there is more profit and sense in going back to sleep with the light off.

Hints for Parents 4: Dealing with nightmares

The best way of handling a nightmare is simply to sit with your child when s/he has calmed down, preferably until s/he is nearly asleep. Do not try to talk about the dream or the anxieties which may, or may not, lie behind it at that time. However, the following day encourage her/him to talk about it, when s/he is feeling relaxed. Do not force the issue if s/he is unable to describe the dream in any detail to you. Simply sharing the fear may help, but you may be able to detect clues in repetitive dreams as to what is troubling them. If the child is too young to articulate their fears, make as little fuss as possible when you comfort them. If s/he feels you are upset and worried, you will only aggravate the problem.